WORLD CELEBRATIONS AND CEREMONIES

Birth

by

Michele Spirn

WORLD CELEBRATIONS AND CEREMONIES

BLACKBIRCH PRESS, INC.
WOODBRIDGE, CONNECTICUT

Published by Blackbirch Press, Inc.
260 Amity Road
Woodbridge, CT 06525

©1999 by Blackbirch Press, Inc.
First Edition

e-mail: staff@blackbirch.com
Web site: www.blackbirch.com

Printed in the United States

10 9 8 7 6 5 4 3 2 1

Photo Credits
Cover and page 10: ©Richard Lobell Photography; pages 3 and 8: ©Charlie Westerman/International Stock; page 5: ©Michael Moody/DDB Stock; page 6: ©H. Rogers/Trip Photographic Library; page 12: ©Michael Lichter/International Stock; page 13: ©Paul J. Buklarewicz; page 15: ©J.P. Courau/DDB Stock; page 17: ©Victor Englebert; page 19: ©Lindsay Silverman/ International Stock; page 20: ©Steven L. Raymer/ National Geographic Image Collection; page 23: ©Peter Russell Clemens/International Stock.

**Library of Congress
Cataloging-in-Publication Data**
Spirn, Michele.
Birth/ by Michele Spirn. — 1st ed.
    p. cm. —(World celebrations and ceremonies)
    Includes bibliographical references and index.
    Summary: Describes how people in various countries around the world celebrate the birth of babies.
    ISBN 1-56711-277-3 (lib. bdg.)
    1. Birth customs—Juvenile literature. [1. Birth customs.] I. Title. II. Series.
GT2460.B5   1999
392.1'2—dc21   98-12117
                                                CIP
                                                AC

☺ CONTENTS ☺

⑥ INTRODUCTION ⑥

In every country of the world, people celebrate when babies are born. Some people have parties. Others go to church for baptism ceremonies. Many people follow customs that they believe will make the baby healthy or lucky. For example, in Japan, fathers fly kites. And in India, an astrologer looks at the position of the stars at the moment a baby was born. As you will see, people in nearly every culture have beliefs about how to ensure good luck and a bright future for their young.

There are different ways of spreading the good news: In Nigeria and in Brazil, people beat on drums to make sure everyone knows about the new baby. In the United States, parents tie balloons to their doors.

All over the world, each baby is important. In some places, a new baby means another person who will help share a family's work and will care for his or her parents when they are old. For every generation, babies are the future. A newborn brings new life and new hope. It also brings a happy promise that the family will live on.

BRAZIL

Most people in Brazil are Catholic, which means they worship in the Christian faith. And like Catholic families all over the world, Brazilian families take their babies to church to be baptized. At a baptism ceremony, a child becomes a Christian like his or her parents. (To learn more about the baptism ceremony, see page 18.)

After a Catholic baby is baptized in São Paulo and in other big cities, parents give a party. Important people who might help the baby later in life are invited, along with friends and family. Most people who come to the party give the baby gifts of silver, which he or she will use as a grown-up.

Many sweet desserts are served at the party. A special one, called "angel's skin," tastes like cotton candy. Another is a coconut candy called *quindim* (KEE-DEE). Children have a separate party. They play games outside and eat candies that are shaped and colored to look like little fruits.

In the northeast, and in many small villages around Brazil,

Key for All Country Maps
★ *Capital city* ■ *Major city*

Brazilians who worship in the Candomblé religion beat drums to announce a baby's birth.

worshippers of the Candomblé religion play drums when a baby is born. They drum to tell their gods about the arrival of the new baby.

In western Brazil, Bororo parents and their new baby do not eat for a few days after the birth. The Bororo think this will help the baby to bear hunger. Being hungry is sometimes part of life for the Bororo people, who live in a swampy region. They hunt for their meat, gather wild plants, and grow corn.

In towns far from the cities, some Brazilians believe it is bad luck to have a bow and arrows in the house when a baby is born. They think that evil spirits might use the bow and arrows to hurt the baby.

ENGLAND

In England, some Christians give newborn babies 12 silver spoons for good luck. Each spoon is shaped like one of the 12 apostles from the Bible. They were men who were chosen by Jesus to spread his teaching. Silver is expensive. When people say, "She was born with a silver spoon in her mouth," they mean she was born to a rich family.

An English mother cuddles her newborn.

The English have many superstitions about birth. Superstitions are beliefs about what causes good luck or bad luck. One belief is that the day of the week on which a baby is born will affect the way he or she looks or behaves. According to an old English poem, "Monday's child is fair of face, Tuesday's child is full of grace…"

England is one of the few countries in the world with a queen. Her name is Elizabeth II. Although she does not govern the country, her position is very important.

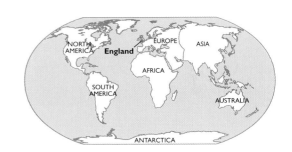

Another idea is that if the baby sleeps on the second floor, it is good luck for the mother to bring the baby downstairs for the first time on a Sunday. But some English people believe that a child who first goes upstairs on a Sunday also will be lucky. So first a mother must carry the infant up to another floor in the house, if there is one. After that, mother and baby come downstairs for a family party.

In the county of Kent, in southeastern England, some families dress their newborn boys in girls' clothes and the baby girls in boys' clothes. This is supposed to fool evil spirits.

Royal births are special in England. When Queen Elizabeth's grandson, Prince William, was born, church bells rang all over England. And in the parks of the capital city of London, soldiers fired guns 21 times in honor of the new prince. Someday, he will be King of England.

INDIA

The Rajput are members of a caste, or group, in India. In Rajput families, a father often chooses a baby's name. Until he does, the baby has a

A Hindu baby has a naming party 12 days after he or she is born.

nickname. A girl is called *Lali* (LA-lee), and a boy is called *Lala* (LA-la). Both names mean "jewel."

In the city of New Delhi and in other parts of India, those who worship in the Hindu religion give a baby a naming party. The party occurs 12 days after the baby is born. Sweets are given to everyone. The baby's aunt—the father's sister—has a special part. She ties red string to the cradle and around the baby's stomach.

She does this to make sure no evil spirits will hurt the baby. Brothers and sisters or other relatives swing the child gently in a red silk *sari* (SA-ree), which is a long piece of cloth. They sing a song that includes the baby's name, which the aunt has chosen.

Many of the Hindu faith, and other people around the world, believe in astrology. It is the study of how stars and planets affect people's lives. In India, Hindu astrologers make special charts for every newborn. The first letter of a baby's name is from the name of a *constellation*, which is a group of stars. Gods or goddesses of India also must be in the baby's first name. In southern India, the father's name is the baby's second name. The child's third name is his or her family's name.

Almost a billion people live in India. That is more people than in any other country except China. The capital of India is New Delhi, in the northern part of the country.

ISRAEL

In Israel there are different ceremonies for Jewish newborn boys and girls. A newborn girl may be brought to a synagogue to be named. On the eighth day after a boy is born, there is a *Brit Milah* (breet mee-LAH). It is a very old ceremony that began with Abraham, the father of the Jewish people. During the *Brit*, the baby is circumcised. That means the fold of skin around the baby's penis is removed. (This is also done regularly in hospitals for many Jewish and non-Jewish babies.)

Then the baby is blessed and named. If the boy is the first-born child, he may also have a *Pidyon Haben* (pid-YON ha-BEN). This ceremony is almost 1,400 years old.

Israel is in a part of the world called the Middle East. The capital of Israel is Jerusalem, which is near the center of the country.

A baby is blessed and named at his Brit Milah.

In the time of the Bible, the first-born sons of some families left their homes and became priests in the Jewish temple. Today, men in these families still act as priests in certain Jewish ceremonies. But there is no holy temple, and the priests live at home. A priest is called a *cohen* (ko-HANE). At a *Pidyon Haben*, friends and family gather 30 days after the baby boy is born. The parents give five silver dollars to a *cohen*. They pretend to "buy" their son back. In doing this, the parents are honoring the days when boys left home to become priests.

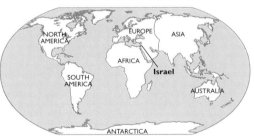

Arab Israelis of the Muslim faith celebrate on the seventh day after a baby is born. Friends and family come to see the newborn. Parents place certain foods around the baby, such as salt, dates, cereal, and sweets. They are symbols of the foods the baby will need to live and grow. The child is blessed by the midwife, a woman who helped at the birth, or by a grandmother. Afterward, guests sing and dance. Muslim boys are circumcised later in life, between the ages of three and five.

JAPAN

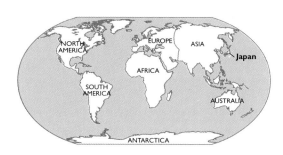

For Japanese who follow the Shinto religion, a baby's first visit to a shrine is very important. A shrine is a holy place. Boys are taken there 32 days after they are born, and girls go 33 days after birth. Babies are dressed in new clothes made by their grandmothers. Mothers carry their infants to the shrine, and other relatives follow her in a line. A priest blesses the baby, and he or she is named.

A mother and baby in the capital city of Tokyo.

Japanese parents give their children names that they hope will bring good luck. A boy might be called *Hideo* (hih-DAY-oh), which means "excellent boy" in Japanese. *Kazuko* (ka-ZOO-koh) is a girl's name. It means "child of peace."

After a trip to a shrine, parents take the baby to see friends and relatives, who give him or her gifts of toy dogs. Some say the dogs are symbols of protection for the baby.

Babies are taken to visit Shinto shrines about a month after they are born.

Back home, after all the visiting is over, a family feasts on fish, rice, and pickles. In Kyoto and other cities, many Japanese celebrate with *tempura* (tem-POO-ruh)—fish and vegetables fried in batter.

Sometimes, a Japanese father flies a kite after the birth of a child. If the kite flies high, Japanese believe the child will have a peaceful, happy life.

⊚ · ⊚ · ⊚ · ⊚ · ⊚ · ⊚ · ⊚ · ⊚ · ⊚ · ⊚ · ⊚

Japan is an island nation in the Pacific Ocean. It is made up of four main islands and many smaller ones. The capital city of Tokyo is on the largest island, called Honshū.

⊚ · ⊚ · ⊚ · ⊚ · ⊚ · ⊚ · ⊚ · ⊚ · ⊚ · ⊚ · ⊚

Mexico

When a baby is born in Mexico, the family often throws confetti, which is cut-up paper. The paper is blue for a boy and pink for a girl.

Mexico is on the continent of North America. The capital of Mexico is Mexico City. It is surrounded by mountains.

A Catholic child is usually named after a holy man or woman called a "saint." Some native groups keep the child's real name a secret and use a nickname instead. They believe that evil spirits could hurt the child if the spirits knew his or her real name.

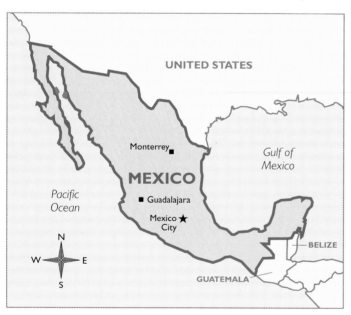

The Tarahumara people in northwest Mexico hold a ceremony a few days after a baby is born. The ceremony is led by an important religious person called a "medicine man." He makes the sign of the cross with a burning torch by moving the torch in four directions. This is to protect the baby from evil. Friends of the family are careful not to say nice things about the infant. They are afraid that if they do, evil spirits may notice the baby and take it away.

Forty days after a child is born, Catholic Mexicans celebrate the *Sacamisa* (sa-ca-MEE-sa). Parents and godparents dress in their finest clothes and take the baby to church. The mother carries the baby into the church first, while the child's father and godparents walk behind. Then a priest blesses the family and the infant. The *Sacamisa* is done to

A Mexican family takes a baby to church for a Sacamisa *at 40 days of age.*

remember the parents of Jesus—Joseph and Mary—who took their son to the Temple of Jerusalem. After the *Sacamisa*, there is a party.

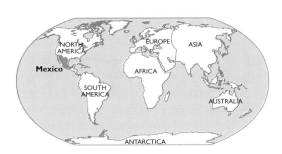

The family may serve *tortillas* (tor-TEE-yas). They are flat breads that are often rolled around chicken or meat. Everyone eats refried beans. Dessert might be fried *tortillas* sprinkled with sugar.

NIGERIA

The Yoruba people live in the city of Lagos and other parts of southwestern Nigeria. When a Yoruba baby is born, no one speaks until the infant is sprinkled with water to make him or her cry. The Yoruba believe this will protect the baby from harm. Then, to make the baby strong and brave and to protect it, the infant is held by the feet and shaken three times.

Mother and baby stay in the house after the birth. If the newborn is a girl, they stay in for six days. But a mother and son stay in for eight days because the Yoruba believe baby boys are not as strong as girls.

On the seventh day, there is a naming ceremony for a girl or a boy. Dressed in her best clothes, a mother sits with her baby near a bowl of water. The father drops money into the water. Then the mother says the name of the baby, which the father has chosen.

Twins are born often to the Yoruba, who have special names for them. The first-born is called *Taiwo* (TAE-woh), which means "younger."

The Hausa beat on drums after a baby is born.

That is because the Yoruba think the baby was sent by the other twin to look at the world. The second twin is called *Kehinde* (KYE-en-dee), which means that he or she "came after."

Other Nigerians have different ways of celebrating the birth of a baby. The Hausa beat on drums to tell everyone about their new children. Christians take their babies to be baptized.

Nigeria is on the continent of Africa. Most people in Nigeria live in small villages. But some choose to live in cities like Abuja, the nation's capital.

PUERTO RICO

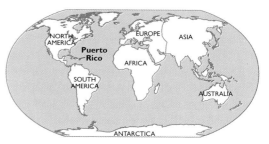

In Puerto Rico, a Catholic family goes to church for a baby's baptism. Catholics worship in the Christian faith. At this ceremony, a baby becomes a Christian. An infant wears a white dress for his or her baptism. The mother holds the baby, and the father stands beside them. A priest sprinkles water over the baby's head and blesses him or her. Then the baby is named.

Before a baptism, parents ask two people to be godmother and godfather. The parents think long and hard about whom they will ask. It is an honor to be a god-parent, but it is also a duty. If anything happens to a child's parents, the godparents must take the child and raise him or her as part of the family.

The first boy in a Catholic family is usually named after his father or his godfather. The first girl might be named after her mother or her godmother.

Puerto Rico is a commonwealth of the United States. That means the people are actually U.S. citizens. But Puerto Rico is independent in many ways. It makes its own laws, or rules.

Atlantic Ocean

San Juan ★

· Mayagüez

PUERTO RICO

Guayama ■

N
W——E
S

Caribbean Sea

Some children's first names are so long, the family uses nicknames. A girl named Losefina may be called Fina. When a family adds *ito* or *ita* to the end of a name, it means "little one" in Spanish. For example, a girl may be called *Carmencita*, or "little Carmen." A boy may be *Jaimito*—"little Jaime."

After a baptism, everyone goes to a baby's home for a festive meal. In San Juan and in other cities and towns, the family may serve a hot dish, such as chicken with rice. Dessert may be *flan* (flahn), which is a sweet vanilla pudding.

In Puerto Rico, Catholic babies are baptized in churches such as this one.

RUSSIA

In the city of Moscow, families of the Russian Orthodox faith may take their newborns to churches such as the Yelokhovsky Cathedral to be baptized. This beautiful cathedral, painted blue and gold, is one of Moscow's most important churches.

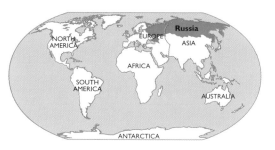

When the Communists were in power from 1917 to 1991, people did not have the freedom they do today. The Communists believed that all land, businesses, and houses belonged to the government. They controlled the people with many rules. A mother and father could lose their jobs if they took their baby to be baptized, because people were not allowed to practice their religion. If a baby's grandmother did not have a job to lose, the parents might ask her to take the baby to be baptized. Now Russia is a democratic country. People can choose to have their babies baptized without being punished.

A Russian Orthodox baby is baptized in a 400-year-old church in Moscow.

The Russian Orthodox belong to the Christian faith. At a Russian Orthodox baptism, the baby is dipped in water three times. If the newborn is a girl, her godmother promises that she will be a good Christian. If the baby is a boy, the godfather does this. Usually the church is filled with flowers. Russians love flowers. They often bring them to parents when a child is born. But they will bring only an odd number of stems, such as one, three, or five. Giving an even number is supposed to bring bad luck.

At a party after a baptism, everyone drinks hot tea with jam. Bread and butter, cheese, and meat are also served. Potato *oladi* (oh-LAH-dee) or cake might be on the table. The *oladi* is made with potatoes, flour, egg, onion, and bacon. It is fried or baked, and Russians eat it with lots of sour cream.

Russia spreads across two continents—Europe and Asia. The land west of the Ural Mountains is in Europe. The land east of the mountains is in Asia.

UNITED STATES

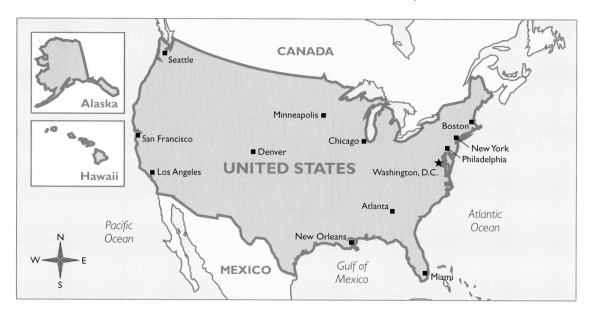

In the United States, parents want everyone to know when a baby is born. They may send out cards to friends and family telling them whether the baby is a girl or a boy. Sometimes the cards are pink for a girl and blue for a boy. Fathers may hand out cigars to their friends. In Washington, D.C., the nation's capital, and in other parts of the country, families tie pink or blue balloons to their doors.

Before the birth, friends and family sometimes give a "shower" for the parents-to-be. The shower is a party where parents-to-be are "showered" with gifts. People give useful gifts for the new baby, such as clothing, plastic dishes, and blankets.

If a baby is born in a hospital, the father will visit the mother and the baby. Sometimes the hospital will let the baby's brothers and sisters come, too. This is a special, quiet time for the family and the newborn.

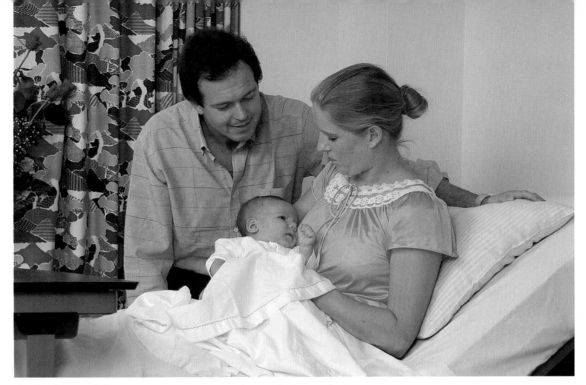

At the hospital, American parents get to know their new baby.

When a baby and the mother come home, friends and relatives come to the house. They bring many gifts, such as stuffed toy animals and rattles. Some may give the baby something with his or her birthstone. A birthstone is a jewel that is a symbol of the month a baby was born. For example, a diamond is for April, and a ruby—a sparkling red stone—is for July. Birthstones are part of an old superstition. People believed these jewels kept an infant safe and brought out the best in him or her. Very few people believe in the power of birthstones today. But they look pretty.

The United States is on the continent of North America. It has large mountain chains near the East and West coasts.

Glossary

astrology The study of how stars, **constellations**, and planets affect a person's life.

baptism A ceremony at which a baby becomes a Christian.

caste In India, a group of people who share the same social position.

ceremony Actions, words, or music that mark a special occasion.

confetti Small, cut-up pieces of colorful paper that are thrown during a celebration.

constellation A group of stars that seem to form the shape of an object, animal, or person.

democratic A system of government that makes sure all people have the same rights and choices.

godparents A man and a woman who promise to look after a child, especially if the child's parents are unable to.

infant A baby or young child.

medicine man An important holy person who is believed to have special powers.

newborn A baby born recently.

superstition A belief about what causes good or bad luck.

symbol An object that represents something else.

Further Reading

Baxter, Nicola. *Babies* (Toppers series). Danbury, CT: Children's Press, 1997.
Ganeri, Anita. *Birth and Growth* (First Starts series). Chatham, NJ: Raintree/Steck-Vaughn, 1994.
Knight, Margy Burns. *Welcoming Babies*. Gardiner, ME: Tilbury House, 1994.
Rushton, Lucy. *Birth Customs* (Comparing Religions series). New York: Thomson Learning, 1993.

Tourism Web Sites

Brazil: http://www.brazilinfo.com
England: http://www.visitbritain.com
India: http://www.tourindia.com
Israel: http://www.goisrael.com
Japan: http://www.jnto.go.jp
Mexico: http://www.mexico-travel.com

Nigeria: http://www.sas.upenn.edu/African_Studies/Country_Specific/Nigeria.htm
Puerto Rico: http://www.Welcome.toPuertoRico.org
Russia: http://www.tours.ru
United States: http://www.united-states.com

Index